MW00799571

Ulysses Cunningham,

A Friend to Man:

The Story of a Soldier & Steward

By Sonia Cunningham Leverette

& Family

Hadassah's Crown
Publishing, LLP

*nothing good happens
without a struggle.*

Ulysses Cunningham

Published by Hadassah's Crown, LLC

Spartanburg, SC 29304

Text Copyright © 2017

All rights reserved. No part of this book may be reproduced, scanned, or distributed in any printed or electronic form or by any means without prior written consent of the publisher, except for brief quotes used in reviews.

Please do not participate in or encourage piracy of copyrighted materials in violation of the author's rights. Purchase only authorized editions.

Library of Congress Control Number: 2017918665

Ulysses Cunningham, A Friend to Man: The Story of a Soldier & Steward

ISBN 978-0-9981230-3-5

Printed in the United States of America

Contents

(Title page photo is Ulysses holding his first great grandson, Jasten Jeremiah (JJ) Franklin, approximately two months old, in November 2016.)

This publication is in memory of
Jannie Watts Cunningham (1901-1995),
virtuous, wise and selfless mother of Ulysses
Cunningham.

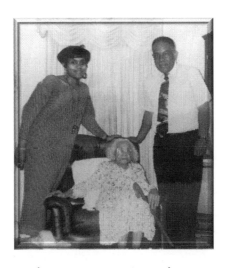

Pictured are Jannie Watts Cunningham, center,

with Ulysses and granddaughter, Sonia on

June 25, 1995 (Jannie's Last Birthday on This Side of Heaven)

Laurens, SC

Ulysses Cunningham, A Friend to Man: The Story of a Soldier & Steward

Introduction

Dr. Sonia Cunningham Leverette

Dad's life belongs in a book. So, a few years ago when he said, "I'd like to sit down and write a book about my life one day," that was the impetus for me to set the ball in motion. I've always imagined the beauty of his life on paper. Both of my parents are those unsung heroes that the world never knows the way it should. But their humility would have it no other way.

While Dad writing a book isn't impossible, it's the sitting down that is. This project has been delayed for an entire year because at the young age of 78, he wouldn't "sit" down. Not for long, anyway. He's managed more pages than I thought, but what you might find in this collection is that his life and character are shown more through the writings of others. Our family and friends, as well as Dad's coworkers, fellow commissioners and church family, have all contributed to bring Dad's goal into fruition.

Of note is that there are some redundancies. Some

sections overlap and repeat portions of Dad's life, but the intent for the use of the information varies. Our prayer is that you will laugh, cry, learn and yearn for more. Dad is as energetic as he was at the age of eighteen, so we look forward to presenting our readers with a sequel.

As you thumb through these pages, you may find that this biography does not follow any traditional pattern. However, you will find the authors and the editors taking liberty to allow readers to view the subject through an array of lenses, far and wide, distant and near. The book does not have to be read cover to cover in the order of the Table of Contents. Enjoy and share it as much as you deem necessary.

We hope this book will inspire and encourage readers of all ages, especially the young with dreams about a better and brighter tomorrow. God bless you for supporting this project; purchasing, reading and sharing this book; for serving your fellow man and for your continued prayers!

"Legacy is not leaving something for people; it's leaving something IN people."

Peter Strople

Ulysses Cunningham, A Friend to Man: The Story of a Soldier & Steward

The Humble Beginnings

Ulysses Cunningham

I was born to sharecroppers on January 1, 1939, the fourth of six children born to Caleb and Jannie Watts Cunningham. My oldest sister, Essie Bee Cunningham Williams, lived from 1924-2012, while my oldest brother, Taylor Cunningham, lived from 1930-1975. My surviving siblings are Otis Cunningham, my middle brother, and my two younger sisters, Evelyn Cunningham Barksdale and Nellie Cunningham Bryson.

Like many boys, I remember being a little on the mischievous side. Otis remembers a few stories about me growing up that he still shares. Once, he sliced hot pepper to season his bowl of corn. He noticed me watching and could tell I wanted a taste. He offered to slice the pepper for me, but I wanted to show my independence and refused his offer. Otis and our other family members watched as I sliced the smallest piece of pepper I could. This small piece would have been considered a "chunk" by many. After I spooned the corn laced with the pepper chunk into my mouth, I immediately began to scream because it was extremely hot. But there was more of a problem. The "chunk" was stuck. It was too hot to move, spit out, or swallow. When Dad realized I was in trouble, he used his finger to remove the chunk of pepper from my mouth. And that story lives on after seventy years.

My father was a good man. He was born in 1899, the oldest son of Caleb, Senior and Hattie Cunningham. Dad had six younger siblings: Cleveland, Richard, Matthew, Annie Bell, MayElla and Minnie. While Caleb lacked education, he was a hard worker. Afraid of debt, he wouldn't buy a house or land. We rented a home and land in order to farm, which served as a means to pay the rent. Caleb believed in church work, and he served as a deacon at my home church, Good Hope Baptist in Waterloo, SC.

One day, when Otis wouldn't stop teasing me, I threw a rock and hit him in the head. Dad made me sit in a bottomless chair while he whipped me across my legs. I don't remember any of my siblings ever getting a whipping from Dad, just me.

Dressing up, especially wearing a necktie, has always been special for me. Casper Williams, my brother-in-law, remembers when Mom purchased me a necktie I refused to wear. Wanting to be older than I was, I insisted that the clip-on tie was for "little boys." Though I was still a little boy, I didn't view myself that way. I wanted a tie I could manipulate. Still today, my wife, Cora, often asks me when I'm going to remove my tie when I arrive home from church. I enjoy wearing dress clothes for as long as I can.

Early Memories

I was born south of Waterloo, SC, on the Saluda River at a place called Rosemont near Cunningham Woods. We moved closer to Waterloo when I was approximately one-year-old and north of Waterloo the next year. We rented a small farm approximately eight acres. This was not enough land to make a living growing cotton and corn. My dad rented more land and worked some land as a sharecropper.

When I was about four years old, I enjoyed going to a one-room, so-called "school." We had one teacher for four grades. While she was teaching one grade, the other three grades were asked to sit still and be quiet until our time to learn came.

At the age of five, I began Laurel Hill School, which was inside a four-room building. I was promoted to second grade prior to beginning at Laurel Hill, but my teacher pushed me back to first grade. My feelings were hurt because I wanted to be with the second graders.

In late summer, my siblings and I would register for school and then miss approximately six to eight weeks to gather cotton and corn. This was required to make a living and to buy books and clothes. Additionally, when we attended school, we walked approximately two miles to school one way.

Maybe once a year, a ten-cent movie, or occasionally a play, came to town or to our school. As an eighth grader,

I volunteered for a speaking contest where I recited the "Psalm of Life" by Henry Wadsworth Longfellow. As second place winner, my reward was five dollars. I remember the pride I felt as though it were yesterday. My love for poetry recitation remains with me today. Some of my other favorite poems include "Myself" by Edgar A. Guest and "Invictus" by William Ernest Henley.

In the spring of each year, we would till the soil in preparation for the planting of cotton and corn. Corn would be planted in early April, while cotton would be planted in mid-April. Some seasons would yield weather that was too cold or too wet for planting. In mid-April through May, we would be free to focus our full attention on the crops.

Sunday morning had its own unique routine, but one thing was certain. It was always time for church. Our lack of a car didn't stop us from traveling the two miles one way. Adorned in our best and following behind our parents, we'd walk to Laurel Hill Baptist Church on Highway 221. After my sister Essie married Casper, he would drive us to Good Hope Baptist Church, which was too far to walk to. This is the same church I am blessed to attend today with my sisters, brother, a few cousins and friends.

As a child, I could never see a future in renting poor land and sharecropping. My vision was to obtain a job on the highway making twenty dollars per week: ten dollars for a house, five dollars for groceries, and five dollars for a car. Three possessions I desired most were a home, car and land.

My aunt Marthella and uncle Matthew only had one child, a girl named Hattie Lee, my double-first cousin. Our mothers were sisters and our fathers were brothers. Aunt Marthella begged my mother and father to allow her and Uncle Matthew to adopt me. Mother refused, but she allowed me to spend many days and nights with their family. Hattie Lee has always been like a sister, and we remain close today.

As a lad, hard work became the norm, but schooling required little effort from me. In grammar school, I was first in my class, graduating as the valedictorian. After completing eighth grade, I began Sanders High School as a ninth grader. As a student bus driver, my salary was twenty-five dollars per month, of which I was quite proud. Daily, I'd park the bus and then fetch the mule and horse to try to find firewood, which was a rare commodity. When I found the wood, it was difficult to cut with an axe. We depended on wood for heating and cooking, and sometimes we depended on the light from the fire for reading.

Though hard work was all my family knew, we did not have the luxuries of a television or a radio, or even electricity, until I was almost eleven years old. There was no bathroom or running water. Our neighbors purchased a television in the early 1950s, and my siblings and I wanted to move in with them. That talking, moving box had new powers of its own, instantly drawing viewers into a world they might never experience themselves or offering concepts beyond the mind's imagination.

During the summer, a baseball team would challenge local opponents on Saturday afternoon, causing my family and me to rush through our cotton picking. Having a quarter meant we could get a hot dog and a Pepsi Cola. Those weren't everyday items, and they were what we looked forward to all week long.

Growing up in the 1940s and 1950s was scary for black people, especially men and boys. I will never forget the story of Emmett Till, hearing about the Ku Klux Klan, as well as the many horrific stories about countless black men and boys. I have a cousin who was involved with a white girl during the early 1950s. His grandfather sent him to Pennsylvania to prevent him from being killed or lynched. Black men and boys were beaten for looking at a white female or for being accused of looking at a white female. My dad often told us stories about black men being lynched by the KKK because they were accused of saying something impolite or for not saying "yes, sir" or "no, sir" to a white person.

My mother told me stories from the 1920s when two notorious plantation owners, Cal Nance and his son, Cal Nance, Jr., terrorized their black workers. One day, my maternal uncle, Willie J. Watts, wasn't feeling well and didn't show up for work on the Nance's farm. Later that day, he was seen down town Cross Hill, SC by Cal Nance, Jr. When asked why he didn't show up for work, Uncle Willie J. told him he didn't feel well. Cal Jr. jumped out of the car to beat Uncle Willie J., but to his surprise, Uncle Willie J. met him with a knife and cut him badly. He came to my parent's home and hid in the loft until dark. Then, someone carried him across the state line into North Carolina, where he made his home in Charlotte. Years later, Cal Jr. was shot and killed by a black man he intended to whip.

Some of the Watts family members were brave, and daring, standing up to anyone. My youngest, maternal uncle, Daniel (Pete) Watts, was discharged from the army after World War II. He was dating a lady who refused to go out with him one evening. When he arrived at the bar, the lady was at the bar with another man. Uncle Pete threatened to slap the lady, but her acquaintance pulled a gun and threatened to shoot him if he did. Uncle Pete ignored the threat and slapped the lady any way. The man shot Uncle Pete and ran. Uncle Pete ran after him with his

knife until he fell dead. This was the first funeral I attended;
I was six years old.

Despite the rampant racism and occasional violence,
life was much simpler then. While we wanted more, we
didn't realize what we had until we were older. What we had
was God, an abundance of love and parents who instilled in
us morals and a strong work ethic. If there was something
we wanted, we had to work hard for it. We were encouraged
to do well in school, treat others justly, live humbly and
forgive others for their offenses. The teachings and
examples of our parents taught us to appreciate whatever
we had and to desire nice things, but we were also taught
not to live lavishly beyond our means and spend
excessively. Saving was a virtue, and our mother was a
miser who made sure needs were met, bills were paid and
the remainder was put away for a rainy day.

After my father passed at the age of 56 from a
massive heart attack, I became the man of the house at
seventeen. My older brothers were grown and living on their

own, so I made taking care of my mother and sisters a priority.

Young Adult Life and Marriage

Sonia Cunningham Leverette

Dad has shared stories about attending South Carolina State University after finishing Sanders High School in Laurens, SC in 1957. A scholarship in agriculture certainly helped with tuition and books, but a full-time job in the dining hall provided meals and boarding. Rising at 4:00 AM and running to the dining hall to assist with breakfast preparation, in addition to serving lunch and dinner, left little time for study outside of class time. Falling asleep while preparing assignments and studying for tests made school life grueling, and Dad's funds and free-time were inadequate. He's told stories about thumbing a ride home, all the way from Orangeburg, SC to Laurens, SC. That was indeed a different time.

Our teachings from Dad are too many to discuss, but a few include turning the other cheek, self-advocating and standing up for yourself. There's a time to fight for your rights. One of the pinnacles of Dad's career at SCSU was his participation in the historic sit-ins during the Civil Rights Movement in 1957 and 1958. With fear in his eyes and knots in his stomach, Dad sat at the counter of S. H. Kress & Company at 946 Middleton Street praying no one would spit on or punch him, or pour hot coffee or a chilly Coca Cola on him. His biggest fear was leaving school with an arrest record, but he set fears aside to stand up for his and African American's rights as first-class citizens.

Dad managed his hectic schedule at SCSU for two years, but then he was drafted to serve in the United States Army. During his two years of service, he was stationed in Fort Gordon, Georgia for six months and Heilbronn, Germany for eighteen months. During this time, the Cuban Crisis occurred with the mission of slowing the Russians down from entering the United States. This was a critically dangerous mission, as Dad and the other soldiers knew they could be captured or even killed.

For leisure, Dad had the pleasure of visiting Paris, France; Barcelona, Spain; Zurich, Switzerland and

Salzburg, Austria. A fond memory is visiting the Geneva Town Hall in Switzerland.

Dad met Cora Lee Burnside (Mom) in the later part of 1960 when they were introduced by dear friends, the late Willie Richardson and his wife Betty White Richardson. Mom's first Christmas gift was a camera. They began dating and kept in touch while Dad was in Germany, as Mom wrote weekly letters. Mom convinced her parents, The Late RB Burnside (born in 1920) and Lois Richey Burnside (born in 1924), to move from Clover Street in Clinton, SC to Second Street in Laurens, SC. Second Street was the same street on which Dad and his sisters Evelyn and Nellie (Net) built a home for their mother. Both homes were on the street behind the lot on which Mom and Dad would later build our home in 1964.

On September 19, 1964 at Grandmother Jannie's home on Second Street, Mom and Dad were married. In 1966, their first daughter, Toni Renee, was born on March 18th. Eleven months later in 1967, their second daughter, Sabrina LaShae, was born on February 11th. The family purchased their first dog, a tan and black male German Shepherd they named King. In 1970, I was born and named Sonia Michelle on May 10th (Mother's Day). The family returned to home from Bailey Memorial Hospital in Clinton, SC, after stopping to purchase snow cones for the three and four-year-olds, on May 12th.

The personal strength Dad gained from participating in the Orangeburg sit-ins gave him confidence to again make history by integrating the cafeteria at 3M (Minnesota Manufacturing & Mining) in Laurens, SC. He and other minorities ate in janitorial closets or restrooms until Dad no longer settled for that type of treatment. At the risk of being fired or disciplined, he one day took his lunch in the cafeteria, sat with some white men, and began eating. Later, one of the men asked him why he would do that. He explained that he had a right to eat in the cafeteria just as anyone else. This was the beginning of a long, productive career with a good, stable company. There would be more uncomfortable racial encounters, but Dad quickly states that his good days outweigh his bad, and he chooses to focus on the better days. His journey was purposeful and all

worthwhile, a part of God's plan.

Dad's Multi-Faceted Career

Toni Cunningham Smith

Dad became a member of Good Hope Baptist Church in Waterloo, SC at the age of 12, where he still attends. He has been a deacon for over 45 years, and he currently serves as Chairman of the Deacon Board. Dad is a member of the Union Number Two Tumbling Shoals Baptist Association, where he served as Chairman of the Program Committee, and he currently holds the position of treasurer. Eager to serve his community, Dad first ran for and was elected to the Board of the Commission of Public Works as a Commissioner in 1992, and he still serves faithfully.

After graduating from high school, Dad attended South Carolina State College from August 1957 to May 1960 where he participated in Army ROTC and majored in Agriculture. Later in 1960, he began working at the Standard Plywood, Inc., in Clinton, SC as a Plywood Grader. In 1961, Dad was drafted into the United States

Army, serving for six months at Fort Gordon, Georgia for

basic training and then eighteen months in Germany. Dad

was honorably discharged from the army in 1963 as a

Specialist Fourth Class (SP4). In 1963, he began his career

at 3M (Minnesota Mining and Manufacturing) Technical

Ceramics in Laurens, SC and remained there for the next

twenty years. Dad started out as a custodian and after just

60 days, he quickly began to climb the corporate ladder. His

next position was a Cast Tape Operator. After serving in

that position for a short while, he became a Quality Control

Supervisor, then Quality Control Auditor, followed by

Dispatcher.

In the mid-seventies, Dad returned to college. This

time he attended Lander University, and finished with a

Bachelor of Science Degree in Business Administration in

1977. In 1983, GE bought the ceramic department from 3M,

and Dad became a Production Control Specialist. When the

company became AlSiMag in 1988, he continued to work as

a in that same position. In 1989, Dad accepted a position at

the General Electric Gas Turbine Plant in Greenville, SC.

His positions there included VPS (Veritas Petroleum Services) Shipping and Receiving, Quality Control Operator, and Gage Lab Technician. He remained at GE until he retired in 1999 as a Quality Control Specialist.

A genuine love for cars led Dad to found Cunningham's Used Cars in 1969, which he still operates today under the name of Cunningham Auto Sales. While we were growing up, Dad sold cars, worked a full-time job, finished college and painted homes on the side. His goal was to buy our first cars, pay for our weddings, give us down payments on our first homes, purchase major appliances and blinds, and even help us pay for our masters' degrees. Dad has been more than a provider and we have always had more than we needed or deserved, but along with the money and gifts came the teachings we needed to learn to manage our money and homes, provide for our children and to support them through college. Though Dad missed his calling of being a teacher, he was a natural and to this day enjoys instilling wisdom in his grands, great-grand and the children of family members, neighbors and friends.

Reflections from the Middle Daughter

Sabrina Cunningham Thomas

Does anyone want to live a life that is long and prosperous? Then keep your tongue from speaking evil and your lips from telling lies! Turn away from evil and do good. Search for peace, and work to maintain it.

Psalm 34 12-14 New Living Translation

These are the words that come to mind when I think about the life that my dad has lived. He set this very example for my sisters and me to live by. Some say that he never meets a stranger; well, he doesn't. He never meets a stranger and he shows genuine respect to everyone he meets. I can recall times when people were disrespectful and downright rude to my father when we were growing up, but he never stooped to their level. His motto is "treat people the way you want to be treated" and that is what he has always done. Actions speak louder than words.

I feel a loss for words when it comes to expressing my love, respect and gratitude for and to my father. Dad is a rare soul. His patience, kindness, and wisdom are all qualities that make him truly unique. He has a love for people that is evident when you see him in the company of someone he has never met before. He listens patiently to what everyone says and makes others feel respected and valued. Dad truly is one of the most Christ-like men I have ever known, and I value his opinion and respect him so.

Some of my fondest childhood memories come from my parents taking us on vacations and trips often. I remember trips to Myrtle Beach, SC; Atlanta, Georgia; Charlotte, NC; Gatlinburg and Pigeon Forge, TN; Niagara Falls and Ontario, Canada; Buffalo, New York; Youngstown and Dayton, Ohio; Baltimore, Maryland; Orlando and Silver Springs, Florida; Philadelphia, Pennsylvania, Detroit, Michigan; New Orleans, Louisiana and Washington, DC, just to name a few. I remember the first time we went to Disney World, shortly after it opened. My sisters and I sang and played all the way to our destinations. Dad had the patience of Job. When his girls would complain about it being hot, or being tired, it was Dad to the rescue. He never wanted us to be uncomfortable or unhappy. He worked hard to make sure we had everything we needed and most of what we wanted, too. I remember Dad studying for college classes, working a full-time job and taking care of the three of us while my mother worked. Again, he had the patience of Job. With our parents, it has always been all about "family."

May 21, 2012

Daddy, I want to let you know how much you are appreciated. You bless the lives of so many people with your selflessness. It's evident why God has blessed you so much. I realize each and every day how truly blessed I am to have been born into such a wonderful and loving family. You have been the best father anyone could have dreamed of having. I love you very, very much!

☺ Shae

Reflections from the Youngest

Dr. Sonia Cunningham Leverette

In my beginning, when Mom and Dad decided to have a third child they were hoping for a boy. They had two girl toddlers. However, since I came along large and healthy, they decided to keep me. If they could manage two girls, they could do three. But this was definitely it. There wouldn't be a fourth shot.

I have pictures of Dad holding me with Toni and Shae close by, and in each he seems to be tickled and thrilled. All our lives when we meet his friends, buddies and coworkers, they always tell us how much Dad talks about and brags on his girls. Well, this comes to us as no surprise. He often fills ours ears with just how proud he is of his girls. He busted his behind working three jobs and sending us to college, but he never complained. His analogy was that he never had to throw away money getting us out of jail, paying for rehab, or paying our bills after we were grown, so his sacrifice was worthwhile. And rarely did he have to force us to study when we were students; we were all motivated to excel. It may be because he often verbalized his regret for not having gone into education that the three of us are educators. We often heard about the power teachers hold to change lives, as well as the advantages of serving in institutions where learning is continuous.

Dad rarely fussed at, or talked to us sternly. When he did, we knew he meant business and he need not have to repeat himself. Once when we were young, but old enough to know better, we decided to play in the two-lane road in front of our home. A neighbor friend served as "the lookout," warning us when a car was approaching. This was new-found fun, or so we thought, until the uncle of "the lookout" drove past. He didn't bother to drive a few more feet, complete a U-turn or even use a neighbor's driveway, he simply backed up the wrong side of the road from where he stopped. After exiting his car, he asked, "Where is Ulysses?" Speechless, we pointed to the door, communicating that Dad was inside the house. He approached the porch, rang the doorbell and proceeded to share his observation while we stood by nervously sweating, eyes the size of golf balls.

Immediately, we were called into the house, spoken to sternly and each spanked on the inside of our palms. We got the message, but we still laugh about that experience to this day. We have often compared the result of this incident to the one where Mom disciplined us after we decided to play in a mud puddle in front of our maternal grandmother's home. That day, we were the recipients of whippings that will forever remain lodged in our minds. Mom wasn't playing, and while we feared both parents, we mostly feared Mom's strong hands and arms. She could strike a mean whip. But Dad's stern lectures were no less effective.

As has been mentioned numerous times earlier, Dad worked three jobs for many years. The repetition of Dad's hard work lets readers know how much we took note and how appreciative we are. In the mid-seventies, Dad returned to Lander College to finish his Bachelor's Degree. I have a fond memory of seeing him study at the built-in kitchen table at night after tucking us into bed. Mom was working third shift. Sharing these stories make me aware of how mischievous my sisters and I were. We had been warned to stay away from the plum tree until the plums were fully ripened. But one day when we were out playing, someone pulled a few plums and started throwing them. After awhile, I decided to rub the debris from one and taste it. It was mighty tart, but it was edible. So, I ate another. And another. And then I lost count. I'm not sure how many I ate, but it wasn't until after bath time and bedtime that my stomach decided it didn't enjoy the plums as much as my palate did, and up they came. For years, Toni, Shae and I slept together. Unfortunately, I slept in the middle of them. So not only was I covered in upchucked plums, so were my sisters. Dad, hearing the commotion, left his studies, and had to begin baths and pajama-picking all over again. But this time, he had a new task. Three heads had to be washed, a brand, new venture for him. Though I was clearly the culprit, he never fussed nor complained.

I don't remember Dad ever styling our hair, but there

was another time he'd have to pay close attention and manipulate my hair. One day when Mom was combing and styling my hair, she noticed a tick clinging to my scalp. She panicked and called my grandmother. They were unable to remove the critter, so they called Dad to come home from work. I remember him arriving and together, he, Mom and Grandmother eliminated the pest that could have caused me extreme illness or death.

Sometimes, I am envious when I see pictures of Dad's taking their daughters to daddy-daughter dances or date night. Those weren't popular during my childhood. But then, I think of all the dates Dad took us on that weren't necessarily labeled as such. There were the trips to the colorful fountain at the fire department on Church Street in Laurens, excursions to pick up snow cones or to The Sweet Shoppe, and one of our favorites was going to visit Dad's painting buddy, Mr. John Calhoun. After turning off our street, South Harper, onto Green Street, there was a hump of a hill just before the train tracks. Speeding along in one of our many Volkswagen's and going down that hill was better than any roller coaster imaginable. While we were spoiled and always wanted to "do it again," I don't recall Dad turning around to travel that road twice. But we looked forward to the next trip to Mr. Calhoun's so we could experience that quickly fleeting thrill.

Weekdays during the summer were exciting. Employees of 3M had access to the company's swimming pool, and Dad would drop us off on his way back to work after lunch. We all received swimming lessons, and two of us learned to swim and even jump off diving boards into the twelve-foot pool. I was the unlucky one, participating in lessons for at least five years. Swimming was just not my thing and I didn't catch on. I blame being traumatized by watching *The Titanic* too early in life. An overly full bath tub could sometimes bring out my aquaphobia.

When I watch young ladies dance with their fathers at cotillions and other formal events, I am deeply touched, as are the other onlookers. While I never was unable to experience this personally, I am reminded of the fond memories of Dad escorting me in homecoming at Laurens

District 55 High School. He was always happy to serve as my driver in the Christmas parades. And then there was the day when he gave me away at my wedding, special memories for sure. We didn't dance on either occasion, but my heart did and does now as I reminisce.

Before I was born, Dad became a used car salesman. Cars and auctions became his favorite pastime. He didn't hang out, play golf or frequent athletic events; he spent his time when he wasn't working, studying or hanging out with family attending auto auctions.

Growing up, our family had a Saturday ritual. We'd rise, eat breakfast, houseclean and watch a few cartoons, but at noon it was time for our weekly trek to Greenville, SC. After a good lunch at Morrison's, Steak and Ale, Ryan's or Golden Corral, Dad would drop us off at the old McAlister Square and he'd head to the auction. There was plenty to explore during the four to five hours he'd leave us. Dinner consisted of nuts and candy from the Peanut Shack or a sugar cone of ice cream from Baskin Robbins.

As children, we never worried about how we would get

back home. Looking back, it was interesting how Dad would

occasionally sell the vehicle we drove to Greenville.

Usually, if he didn't make a purchase, he'd borrow a car from

another dealer. We'd ride three deep in the front and three

deep in the back. Grandma Lois was not going to miss a

Saturday shopping trip. Sometimes, Dad would buy two or

three cars, and we'd divide up. Toni might ride with Dad,

Shae might ride with Mom and I always wanted the most

interesting experience, riding with Grandma. She'd say she

couldn't see at night, her glasses weren't working and "Oh,

did that light just turn red? Well, I'll be dog gone!" She

wasn't allowing Mom or Dad to leave her sight because she

claimed she didn't know the way home. Danger didn't enter

my mind; I enjoyed laughing until my overly full tummy

ached.

I recall a sad night. We picked up a mentally

challenged girl who seemed abandoned; she had a moped

and was stranded at the gas station near the auction. She

was sitting alone and crying. Dad asked her how he could

help her, and she said she couldn't get home. The two of

them struggled to lift her moped into the trunk, and she gave us directions to her home. I was sad because the girl seemed so sad. The house she identified as home had no lights on, and it appeared no one was home. She simply disappeared walking toward her home. It was very late when we got home, but that would not stop neither of us from attending church the next morning.

Ecclesiastes 1:18, in the New International Version, states "For with much wisdom comes much sorrow." On the night I just described, I grew wiser while experiencing sorrow for this girl whose name I never knew. What I learned from Dad is that when we see a need, we assist. While we might be unable to heal a wound or pay an electricity bill, we can find some way to help if we truly care. Did it matter that the girl was a total stranger? Absolutely not. Did it matter that it was already late or that the moped was heavy and didn't exactly fit in the trunk? Not at all. This memorable experience was just one of many that not only demonstrated how much of a humanitarian my father is, but that there is an expectation from me. If there is a need I can meet, if I can make life better for someone or if I can assist someone along the way, the concept of serving others has been not only instilled within me but ingrained.

Looking back, work never seemed stressful for Dad. He was always a happy, positive person, singing in the mornings, speaking the little German he remembered, or sometimes reciting poems and expecting us to recall the poet. Growing up we never remembered. But we would later learn that Dad had many stressful situations on the job.

Looking back, each of my sisters and I loved spending time with our dad, until we began liking boys. Dad took us on many dates, many simple and inexpensive, yet more meaningful than words can express. He'd let us tag along to explore new territory when he painted homes, or when he went to purchase cars. And Dad's love could turn a dark encounter into a fond memory.

Once when we visited a home less than ten miles from ours to look at a Volkswagen, the home owner opened a fence, allowing about six full-sized German Shepherds out. As a five-year-old, I immediately took off running in the opposite direction. Fearfully looking back to see how far away the canines were, I ran into a tree. Now lying on the ground watching these same animals salivating over me, I felt one ripping the bottom of my pants with his teeth. But before I could slip into unconsciousness, Dad was right there scooping me up into his arms. The look of fear on his face exceeded what I felt, and though I'd just experienced a traumatic event, I've chosen to cling to his love and protection instead. But my love and protection for him caused me even as a child to have more empathy for him than for myself. After all, he had to face Mom and explain why my beautiful, new outfit was now shredded like lettuce at the bottom.

Generosity is no stranger to my Dad. My sisters and I always had nice, used cars, and I admit a couple times I was greedy. My first car was a 1982 two-door, manual shift, metallic blue Datsun 200SX with leather seats. It was sporty with silver wheels and a silver luggage rack on back. Just as cute as a button! I drove it for a while and was so satisfied, until I laid eyes on a brown one with beige cloth seats. What really caught my attention about the brown one was that it talked...."the door is ajar"...."the key is in the ignition"...."the trunk is open." Now that was cool beans to me! I had to have it; I rode by the car lot every day.

Apparently, I begged enough. One day, I had gone with my grandmother to grocery shop for our home, as I often did. I wanted to help my mom out by taking some responsibilities off her plate. So, my grandmother and I had a Thursday afternoon ritual of going to Bi-lo. Well, lo and behold. When I pulled into the driveway, Dad was rinsing off my new car and Mom was watching. They hadn't let me in on their secret plans to upgrade my car. I immediately exited my car, jumped up and down and ran and grabbed and hugged them both. I was tickled beyond pink to something darker than fuchsia.

Looking back, it was selfish to become fixated on that car. My sisters were in college and it wasn't easy for my parents to take care of their tuition, room, meals and spending. And my sisters even shared a car, which called for lots of sacrificing on the weekends.

But my greedy, self-centeredness didn't stop there. In my defense, Dad was the first to see another car two years later and commented on how pretty it was. Although it was over thirty miles from our home, I just had to drive by. And, it was love at first sight. I found myself begging, again! This was a 1984 white, Toyota Celica with blue sports stripes. After I wore Dad down with my begging, I soon became the owner of my third car after having been a licensed driver for just over two years.

Dad loved cars, and so did we. But new cars have been a rarity in our family. Avoiding the initial depreciation has outweighed the new car smell. Dad's philosophy is if you do your homework right and "smell them over well enough," you can buy a good one that can take you hundreds of thousands of miles and save you lots of money.

My sisters and I all chose sports cars upon college graduation; it was the candy apple red Nissan 300ZX for Toni, a candy apple red Mazda RX7 for Shae, and a metallic blue Toyota Supra for me. Our parents assisted with our weddings, down payments on our homes, appliances and even kept our children for a few years after they were born. This was even with them working full-time. Their sacrifices have been never-ending. Our first financial advisor was Dad. Whenever we were ready to move out on our own, he was happy to sit down with us for budget preparation, making sure we wouldn't find any surprises. He'd instilled in us that it isn't always what you make, but it's what you make of it. Living within your means and saving are both important. Even as educators, life has been good, despite the naysayers who scoff at teacher's salaries. None of us stopped after our Bachelor's Degrees; we went on to earn Education Specialists and Doctorate Degrees, as well as National Board Certification.

Our parents have always instilled within us that we should treat people right regardless as to how they treat us. As entrepreneurs, neither of them sought wealth at the hands of their customers. Customer service was always first, and that has led to an almost fifty-year car business for Dad with numerous repeat customers, and Mom retired from the hair business after thirty years. She ended her career with most of the same faithful customers she began with.

My sisters and I have had tremendous examples of selfless service set before us. In the early 1990s when our paternal grandmother fell ill and needed extra assistance, Dad was there to help. He and his siblings rotated, and Mom often sent meals. There was no sacrifice Dad wouldn't make for Grandmother.

While caring for a parent is often expected, Dad didn't stop there. He assisted his aunt in taking care of her adult, disabled son, Ossie Bee, for many years. And when his Aunt Bessie was stricken with Alzheimer's, Dad was her primary caretaker. For years, he assisted her with all her needs and he allowed her to stay in her home for as long as possible. When her safety from being alone at night was compromised, Dad always sought the best nursing homes for her and worked closely with the staffs. When Aunt Bessie was unable to remember or trust other close relatives, a commonality of Alzheimer's patients, she never lost trust in Dad. She knew he would be a good and honest steward over any and everything she owned, and she couldn't have been more correct.

About four years ago, life changed for Mom and Dad. Our maternal uncle, Johnny, suffered from lung cancer, and they became his and our maternal grandmother's caretakers. Daily, they would prepare meals and drive Johnny to chemotherapy. After he passed, Grandmother could no longer live on her own. She had been found on the floor too many times, having fallen and being unable to reach anyone. Our parents took Grandmother in without hesitation, and they have dedicated these last few years to taking care of her. Never have we heard them whine about missing vacations, visiting our homes or having the freedom to do whatever they want when they want. Our parents are in great health and could lead much more active lives, but they are dedicated to the priority of taking care of family. This value has been instilled in us time and time again. Our parents selflessly reared us, assisted with our children and continue to take care of their last parent. Saying and doing are totally different words; throughout life, our parents have shown us far more than they could ever tell us.

Interview with Dad

Sonia: What is your favorite color?
Dad: Blue

Sonia: Any particular shade?

Dad: Dark or navy blue

Sonia: You're a Capricorn. Do you read much into your

Zodiac sign?

Dad: No, I haven't read much into that.

Sonia: What is your favorite scripture?
Dad: Isaiah 6:1-3

[1] In the year that King Uzziah died I saw also the Lord sitting upon a throne, high and lifted up, and his train filled the temple.

[2] Above it stood the seraphims: each one had six wings; with twain he covered his face, and with twain he covered his feet, and with twain he did fly.

[3] And one cried unto another, and said, Holy, holy, holy, is the Lord of hosts: the whole earth is full of his glory.

Sonia: What is your advice to young people today?

Dad: Be very mannerly and read, read and read. A

person should read everything in sight,

definitely scripture, then newspapers and

literature of all genres. Don't skip over words—

learn those you don't recognize. Tell the truth.

Live so you don't have to lie and exaggerate.

Sonia: Do you have any regrets in life?

Dad: **A lot. I would read more and be more serious in**

school. I'd think before speaking. I would have

been saved much sooner. I would have stayed

away from the vices of the world, and I would have

finished South Carolina State University. When I was

younger, I wanted to be a

math teacher or an army officer, but I enjoyed my

career. Production control was dearer to me

than quality control, but both were great.

Also, I would have given my wife of 53 years more

credit for her hard work and support of me, especially

when I worked 15 to 18 hour days. I did not realize

how much work and how hard it was for her to keep

up our household while I was away. Sometimes my

job required me to visit vendors in New York, Virginia

and other states. When I was in school, Cora worked

second shift at 3M. She would arrive home at 12:30

AM and lay out your and your sisters' clothes for the

next morning. She'd rise early to dress you all, feed

you and drive you to school. My lunch was prepared every day, and the house was always well-kept. Cora even assisted me with yard work, and she could always make it look neater than me. It wasn't until I retired in 1999 that I realized just how much work goes into keeping up a house.

Sonia: When did you get saved?

Dad: At Good Hope about 25 years ago.

Sonia: Is there anything not included in the book you'd like to mention?

Dad: Not really. Well, yeah. I'd rather for someone hurt my feelings than for me to hurt someone else's feelings. I'd rather be intimidated than to intimidate someone.

Sonia: What are your favorite sayings?

Dad: "You will reap what you sow." "Your sins will find you out.

Tributes,

Letters

& Writings

Tributes

Ulysses is truly an example of what a husband, father and human being should be. The 53 years of marriage we've shared have quickly slipped upon us.

Cora Burnside Cunningham -- Wife

Ulysses is a sweet, loving son. I don't have a son-in-law. He's my son and I love him, love him, love him. He treats me like a mother and there's nothing he wouldn't do for me. I feel the same way about him."

Lois Richey Burnside – Mother-In-Law

Man of the SPIRIT of GOD

Marvin W. Smith

I first want to start off by giving all praise and honor to "GOD ALMIGHTY," the Creator of all things. I have met some honorable men in my life and I am quite certain that these men received their good character and honor through having a long and faithful relationship with GOD. I have had the awesome pleasure and blessing through GOD to meet the most amazing Man I have ever known and am certain will ever meet.

Mr. C. exemplifies, in my opinion, all of the fruits of the SPIRIT of GOD mentioned in Galatians 5: 22, 23. (22. But the fruit of the Spirit is love, joy, peace, long-suffering, kindness, goodness, faithfulness, 23 gentleness and self-control.) His love is illustrated in the way he loves his wife, children, grandchildren and everyone he encounters. His joy is typified in the satisfaction he gets from helping others. His peace is personified by the way he treats everyone with passion and grace. His longsuffering is shown in the patience that he shows in dealing with others. His gentleness is represented in the way he conducts his life toward those he loves most. His goodness is exemplified by generosity to all, while his faith is epitomized in his service to his GOD as well as his church. His meekness is embodied through his gentle and quiet nature, and his temperance is demonstrated in the behavior in which he treats everyone. I love Mr. C. for the man he is and the honorable example he has shown me. Mr. C. is a Man of the SPIRIT of GOD.

Dad and Marvin
Christmas 2014
Simpsonville, SC

A Faithful Father

John Timothy Thomas (Skeet)

The Bible says that a godly father is a blessing to his family. *"The righteous man walks in his integrity; blessed (happy, fortunate, enviable) are his children after him"* (Proverbs 20:7, *AMP*). The Bible describes him as the glory of his children (Proverbs 17:6). Although the world has a distorted image of fatherhood, a faithful father obedient to God's will is the cornerstone of a strong family. Being the head of the family is the job of a lifetime.

Our heavenly Father sets the perfect example through His Son, and fathers everywhere can't go wrong but will benefit by taking to heart lessons from the Bible. *"My son, despise not the chastening of the Lord; neither be weary of his correction: For whom the Lord loves he corrects; even as a father the son in whom he delights"* (Proverbs 3:11, 12). In ancient Greece when students were given to a teacher or mentor, they were given what's called a *Hupogrammos, which means "imitation."* This was essentially a writing tablet or copy stencil that was given to children to copy, both as a writing exercise and as a means of impressing a moral.

I am not a biological son of Mr. Cunningham's but he has treated me as one for the past 30 years. I have come to honor, love and respect him as I do my own father. The wisdom, counsel, advice, and guidance I have received from him when I needed answers have served me well. Mr. C. has always been the one I can count on in good times and bad. He has chosen to walk along God's path and the Bible assures him that he won't slip or fall. I, too, as a son, and student now follow his lead. Whether cradling his newborn grandchildren in his arms, to teaching them respect and good manners, walking his daughters down the aisle, or being a grandfather, he knows God will never leave him.

Mr. C. sees honor in not only taking care of his own family, but those outside of it who may need help as well. In doing so, he has instilled in me something very precious and worthy of honor—the image of a loving father. I am forever grateful for the lessons

learned and imparted into my life.

Dad and Skeet
Summer 1997
Disney World, Orlando, Florida

To My Beloved Father-in-Law

Minister Barry Thompson Leverette

Grace, mercy, and peace from God the Father and Christ Jesus our Lord. I am writing to express my love for you and how you have accepted me as a son-in-law. When I think about all the good things God has given me, I am reminded of you. Your wisdom is far better than the treasure of silver and gold. It is sweeter than honey and finer than wine, brighter than the sun and to be loved more than precious stones.

You have taught me to trust in the Lord and your courage has shown me how to walk in faith. I am reminded of Moses who kept the flock of Jethro, his father-in-law, the priest of Midian: and he led the flock to the backside of the desert, and came to the mountain of God, even to Horeb, flailing because of guilt. When the burdens of this old world have me cast down, you are there to restore my circulation and so I can move again. You are a loving Shepherd, Mr.

Cunningham, there with His grace. You hold me there until I have gained my spiritual equilibrium. You are my David and Moses all in one. I can hear you say, "Hold on son; I am here to restore your mind (the third eye of Heru), heart and soul." This is what every shepherd would understand.

As I end this letter of appreciation, it is never goodbye because we do not have a spirit. We are a spirit. Long live Mr. C., my Beloved shepherd. May God sustain your soul until your energy transfers back to the Most High. And may the ancestors guide you on this earthly, spiritual journey.

Dad and Barry
December 2008
Anderson, SC

What Is A Hero?

Chris Merrill, First Grand

(Assignment Completed in Sixth Grade, Bryson Middle School, Simpsonville, SC)

A hero is someone who has character. A hero is someone who is nice to everyone, and has a good heart. He thinks about other people instead of himself. He is not selfish and greedy and is always willing to share. My hero is my grandpa. He is willing to give people money when they need it the most. He is always willing to help and have a good personality.

These were my thoughts as a sixth grader. These are still my thoughts today as a 27-year-old man. My grandfather, Ulysses Cunningham, is by far the kindest man I know. I aim and aspire to be like him.

There are other characteristics I would like to add to my sixth grade list. My grandpa is very knowledgeable, extremely hardworking, and exceptionally honest. He has displayed these characteristics my entire life, and that's why he was my hero growing up, he is my hero now and he will

always be my hero.

Papa and Chris
Disney World, Orlando, Florida
July 1995

My Love for My Papa

Jasmine Aleyshia Thomas, Second Grand

My love for my papa and the love he has for me has always been unconditional. I don't think I could ever think of one time he has ever yelled at me and my sibling as kids! He has always been the person with the calmest demeanor I have ever met in life. I mean seriously, no matter the situation, no matter how many times others are unkind to him, he always is so sweet and loving back. I would love for my future husband to be like him personality wise because I know I could never go wrong with a man like him! Anytime I have ever needed him he has always been there for me no matter what time I call, especially for my car needs! I don't know anything about a car, especially when it comes to fixing one, but I know he's one person I can rely on to have me up and rolling again!! I just want to wish him the best and I pray he enjoys every day he has on this Earth. I want him to know I appreciate his kindness, his love, gratitude, and

everything he has done for our family and me.

Papa and Jasmine
March 1995
Laurens, SC

Courage

Bryant Scott Cheek, Jr. (BJ)
Third Grand
(Written in English III at T L Hanna High School, Anderson, SC)

Courage, faith, hope, selflessness, dedication and tenacity are just a few of the characteristics of college students participating in sit-ins during the Civil Rights Movement. This was just one of the selfless acts of service my grandfather, Ulysses Cunningham, committed. I call my grandfather "Papa" because he is like a dad to me. Because of Papa's diligence and selflessness, I am the person I am today.

Papa is influential to me because he served in the military for several years. He entered the army during a time when African Americans were often mistreated by officers and by their peers as well. He tells stories of being punched in the stomach and barely escaping racially-motivated shootings in German bars. I cannot even imagine what my grandfather went through. Veteran's Day warms my heart knowing Papa is a veteran and is still with us today.

Another reason I am proud of my grandfather is because he graduated from Lander College. He originally attended South Carolina State University (SCSU), a historically black university, but he left due to a lack of money. For as long as he could manage, he worked in the dining hall for eight hours a day, then attended classes and studied. One can only function for so long without sleep, so he left SCSU after two years. And even though he was in "survival mode," he found time to advocate for the state of African Americans by risking his life and participating in sit-ins in S.H. Kress & Company in Orangeburg, SC in 1958. Papa persevered and received a degree in Business Administration in 1976, and he influenced me to go to college and graduate. Papa always tells me, "BJ, do what you have to now, so you can do what you want to do later."

Barbara Bush once said, "You have to love your children unselfishly. That is hard. But it is the only way." This quote describes my grandfather because he was and still is very unselfish. Grandpa worked three jobs to support his family, even when he attended college. He made sure my mother, her two sisters, and my grandmother had everything they needed, and he put my mom and aunts through universities, leaving no debt behind. In addition, he helped them pay for their Masters' Degrees, bought them nice cars, paid for their weddings and receptions, gave them down payments on their first homes and even purchased their first appliances. These are huge accomplishments for a man who grew up in extreme poverty, the son of sharecroppers and the grandson of slaves. Papa continues to serve his community today by serving on the Commission of Public Works in Laurens, SC. He is one of two African Americans serving in this capacity for over 20 years.

To graduate from college, serve in the military, and to be a great father are accomplishments. Amazingly, to serve the country and to participate in the Civil Right's Movement, on top of Papa's other accomplishments despite every adversity against him, are highly commendable acts of service. I am very proud of my grandfather, and I work hard every day so he will also be proud of me one day.

Papa and BJ

June 2001
Myrtle Beach, SC

May 2010
Anderson, SC

My Grandfather

Bryant Scott Cheek, Jr. (BJ)
(Written in English 101 at Limestone College, Gaffney, SC)

Some people grow up without their grandparents. I, however, have been blessed enough to have all of mine still. But I would like to write about my mom's dad. His name is Ulysses Cunningham and he stands five foot eight inches. Even though he is light skin and I am dark, we have the same blood and that is all that matters. My grandfather graduated from college and he also served in the military. I wouldn't be the hardworking person I am today if it wasn't for my grandpa.

My grandfather has been very influential to me in my life. He served in the military for many years. The reason he went to the arm is to serve the country and to make money for his family. In the military, you work extremely hard to protect the country. I cannot even imagine what my grandfather went through in his training to be in the military. Every time I work out or go through a hard practice, I just think about how much harder he had to work. That is why I try to work hard when things are tough. For anyone to serve our country is amazing, but for my grandfather to serve means a lot to me.

Lander College, now Lander University, is where my grandfather graduated from. He influenced me to go to college and graduate. My grandfather always tells me, "BJ, do what you have to now, so you can do what you want to do later." He had to work full time while going to Lander. For most, it is already hard enough to go to school, but to have a full-time job while going to school had to be really rough. Anytime I get down because football and school seem overwhelming, I just try to remember how it would be to have a full-time job. I am lucky to be able to play a sport that I love instead of having to work for money so I can eat.

My grandpa and grandma had three children. After grandpa graduated from college, he worked three jobs to support the family. He made sure my mother and her sisters had everything they needed. He put my aunts Shae and Toni through the University of South Carolina and my mother through Clemson University. My grandpa made sure that when they graduated, they did not have any loans to pay. Now by saying that I am not bragging, but that shows how hard he had to work because college is very expensive.

To graduate from college, serve in the military, and be a great father is a lot. My grandfather tells me every time I see him, "Work hard in school so you don't have to work for anyone for cheap." My grandpa has had his own car dealership for a long time now. By him having his own car dealership, one day I want to have my own gym for fitness. Yes, it will be a lot of hard work, but hard work is the only thing I have ever been taught by him. He does not do it for the money, but to survive you have to make money. I am very proud of my grandfather, and I work hard every day so he will also be proud of me.

A Role Model

Jalen Christopher Thomas
Third Grand

What makes a role model? I believe the words of the late great Albert Schweitzer puts it best, "Example is Leadership." That quote best describes my grandfather, Ulysses Cunningham. Not only has he been an exemplar of leadership in my life, but also to others that have been blessed to meet and to know him. He is a man who thoughtlessly humbles himself and he is not afraid of generosity. Never have I seen my grandfather not be generous, a kind of generosity that could have only been obtained through a bold man trusting in the Lord above."...*for the Lord loves a cheerful giver.*" **2nd Corinthians 9:6**. It's a generosity I wish to situate into my own life. My grandfather has been through what seems to be all walks of life; from being in the army and traveling the world, working on a farm as a sharecropper in the South, working in the factories and working in auto sales (To which

I have benefited much from). Much wisdom has been ascertained by my grandfather through the eventful life he has lived and to my surprise, he's delighted to share whatever he has learned with anyone at a moment's request. I have learned much from him. "What you can learn in a conversation with an elder in an hour, you would have learned reading books in a hundred hours." – *Native American Proverb*. My grandfather is a man of great virtue, has a work ethic unparalleled and a love for family that is to be admired. I love my grandfather and I thank God that he is such a wonderful man and a truly positive role mode. Thanks Papa.

Papa and Jalen
January 2005
Laurens, SC

My Special Memory

Evelyn Cunningham Barksdale
Younger Sister

While in school, we were not as fortunate as some other children. This was a motivation for Ulysses to strive for a better life. As a teenager, Ulysses wanted to earn his own money. He drove a school bus when he was in high school. After finishing high school, he worked at the Plywood Plant. He wanted to work hard and buy a house. He was not satisfied with having to live in a rented house. In 1960, he accomplished his dream without help. We were able to move into a new house, which we were buying and not renting. His hard work paid off and he has been successful in his efforts.

Note To Ulysses From Evelyn

Thank you for being the best brother one could have. You have always looked out for us from our early childhood up to the present time. We are always calling on you for one thing or another, and you always come to our rescue without hesitation. Life would not be the same without you. Not only do you help the family, you are always lending a helping hand to others. You are one in a million. I am proud to be your sister.

My Special Memory

Nellie Cunningham Bryson (Net)
Youngest Sister

When we were growing up, I remember you always had dreams of owning farmland. Our family worked on rented farmland. We did not own anything of our own and you had visions of getting out of poverty, living like the middle class. You dreamed of getting a job on the highway where you could earn $20 per week so you could pay $5 on a house, $5 on a car, $5 living expenses and $5 for savings. As you grew up, you worked hard to make sure your dreams became reality.

Note To Ulysses From Net

I am so proud to have you as a brother. You have helped me in so many ways. Not only have you helped my family and me, you go out of your way to help others. You have an extraordinary reputation, which you have so graciously earned. When I meet people who know you, they always comment on what a nice person you are. I have to agree with them. It's not every day one can find such an amazing person. Thank you for who you are and all the good things you do.

Tribute to Our Uncle

Dorothy Williams (Dot)

Our mother, Uncle Ulysses' oldest sister, said she could not ask for a better brother. My sisters, Barbara and Janet, and I couldn't ask for a better uncle. He is a kind, soft-spoken man, but he is no joke. Uncle Ulysses will tell you the truth whether good or bad. That is just one of many good traits we admire about him. Uncle Ulysses has always been like a second dad. He keeps the oil and tire pressure checked in my cars. If something happens to my car, Uncle Ulysses will always let you borrow one of his. Uncle Ulysses will do anything he can to help anyone, and you know when he does it he really doesn't mind.

Uncle Ulysses has always been there for us over the years. When we were younger, one of us would follow him around when we would visit our grandmother. He would be target practicing and he would let us shoot his gun. Our uncle was the person who taught us to parallel park, park on a curb and park on a hill. We would not have gotten our licenses had it not been for Ulysses instructing us.

During one of the driving excursions, Uncle Ulysses took one of us to prepare for the driving test. This sister wishes to remain nameless. When she was instructed to back up, she backed up and hit a pole. She laughed and said, "But you didn't tell me to look back." She said, "Uncle Ulysses just said, 'I guess we will go home now.' She said anyone else would have gotten angry, but he was just as calm as ever. Uncle Ulysses has the patience of Job. We have never seen him lose his temper. He has always been someone to look up to for the way he treats family, friends and acquaintances.

Once when Mother was terminally ill and had fallen, we didn't know how we were going to get her back in bed. Suddenly, the doorbell rang and it was Ulysses. It was if God had sent him. He picked her up and put her back in bed. Also, during this time, he would come over and vacuum and mop. One could not imagine how much this helped.

Ulysses Cunningham, A Friend to Man: The Story of a Soldier & Steward

Uncle Ulysses is an example of how a Christian should live and conduct himself. It is just too bad the world is not made up of more people like Uncle Ulysses.

My Cousin Ulysses

Leon Bennett

Ulysses and I grew up in the same small community of Laurens County called Waterloo, SC. We walked a dirt road in order to play together. When we finished school, I moved to Detroit, Michigan. Later, Ulysses went to the army. Even though we were miles apart, we kept in touch. Whenever I would visit my hometown, I'd always visit Ulysses and his family.

I moved back to my hometown in 1989 because of my mother's illness. I would talk to Ulysses or visit him often. Today we are both retired and check on each other daily. We will help each other in any way we can. Besides being cousins we are best friends.

Dear and Beloved First Cousin

James E. Fuller

I'll begin with just a brief history of our close relationship. As young boys, there was a slight difference in our ages. Therefore, at the time Ulysses would pal around with my two older brothers. As we grew older and developed some of the same interests, we communicated and associated more. We both got married in September of different years, but our anniversaries were days apart.

On two occasions, we traveled to Gatlinburg, Tennessee and Hilton Head, South Carolina where we spent an entire week together. While our wives shopped, Ulysses and I had long periods of conversation. I can only say good things about my cousin Ulysses because of the great example he sets for others to follow, especially the example he sets for young men. Ulysses possesses such a quiet and easy spirit that one can't help but like him. I have never heard a bad thing said about him, nor can I say anything negative about my cousin. I personally have always found him to be friendly, caring, helpful and trustworthy.

On a more personal note, our Aunt Bessie Watts Justice was stricken with Dementia. Ulysses, along with his family, took on the responsibility of primary caretakers. After the passing of our Aunt Bessie, I was later faced with that same role of caretaker for my mother (again Ulysses' aunt). By Ulysses having previously served as a caretaker, he was a great support for me, both as a listening ear as well as a GREAT source of advice. He at that time became my rock and a pillar of strength. My brother Cornell, who passed in August of 2013, had been my support system. After losing the last of my two brothers, I consider Ulysses to be my Cousin/Brother and Friend.

A Special Cousin

Lessie L. Watts

Ulysses Cunningham continues as a successful businessman, a productive community leader, a devoted family man, proud father and grandfather. He serves the deacon board of his church, and he's well-known and active in the community. He assists in selecting and distributing funds to the sick and needy of the community.

In all his endeavors, Ulysses uses the highest of morals and integrity. Ulysses Cunningham continues to be dependable, trustworthy, and he uses his abilities and resources to go the "extra mile" whenever his services are needed. His work shows patience and preparation.

Interview of a Change Agent

Minister Tony Cunningham

A change agent is someone who brings about, or helps to bring about, a change. The individual that I chose to interview for my change agent is Mr. Ulysses Cunningham. Mr. Cunningham is a native of Laurens County, South Carolina. He was born into poverty in the town of Waterloo, SC in 1939. Growing up as a sharecropper, he spent many hours in the cotton fields earning a wage of two dollars a day. Having to work all his life to achieve and to become an overcomer, Mr. Cunningham had to endure the role as the male leader of his family after the passing of his father when he was in the eleventh grade. Mr. Cunningham attended South Carolina State University in 1957, and after facing financial difficulty, left college after only two and a half years. In 1960, he led the building of a home for his family in Laurens, SC at the age of 21. In 1961, he was drafted into the United States

Army. Mr. Cunningham served 18 months in Europe, where he excelled in his field and grasped his leadership abilities.

Carrying the role of the man in the family helped shape him into the leader he is today. When Mr. Cunningham returned home from the military, he was offered a job as a janitor at a plant in Laurens. He refused the janitor's job. After being called back in by the plant manager and being told about how the company had to hire blacks, Mr. Cunningham later accepted the job. Afterward, he was offered a job in production. He discovered his purpose as a leader and developed a willingness to stand for what was right while working at the plant in Laurens. A co-worker who was white and Mr. Cunningham went into the lunchroom to eat their lunch. Being one of a few blacks in the company, when Mr. Cunningham walked into the lunchroom, the whites walked out in protest of him being there. He was questioned as to why he came into the lunchroom to eat instead of going into the janitor's closets with the other blacks. Mr. Cunningham told his co-worker of all the things he had been through to get where he was, and that nobody was going to tell him where he could and could not eat. He stated that it was not a company policy, and he began to encourage the other blacks to eat where they had a right, and that was in the company lunchroom. By speaking out, he helped integrate the company's lunchroom. Mr. Cunningham moved from janitor to a Quality Control Supervisor, where he supervised 24 individuals. This offered him the opportunity to hire other qualified blacks, all within a four-year time span. There were still obstacles he had to face. Salary discrimination was evident against him and other blacks. It was hard to gain loans from banks. It was hard for some co-workers to accept him as a supervisor.

In 1973, Mr. Cunningham went back to college to obtain his degree in Business Administration from Lander College. This allowed him to make an above average salary. The most significant contribution he has made to his community is his daughters. He put three daughters through college. His daughters impact the lives of others daily, serving in public education for a combined total of nearly ninety years. One of his daughters is an author and has a doctorate degree in education.

There are many lessons that can be learned from Mr. Cunningham's life. You can learn how to appreciate the little things in life. One of his memorable quotes from his mother was "If you work harder than the average person, you can have more than the average person by being responsible, wisely managing, and earning an honest living." Mr. Cunningham is a man who waits on nobody to give him anything. If you want it, you've got to earn it. During the time I spent with Mr. Cunningham I also learned that no matter what you do there is always going to be critics. Even in the midst of chaos, always try to do what is right.

Mr. Cunningham is retired from General Electric, serves on the Board of Directors for the Laurens Commission of Public Works, and is currently the Chairman of the Deacon Board at Good Hope Baptist Church in Waterloo, SC. I asked Mr. Cunningham how he views leadership in organization. He responded with a serious look, square in my eyes and said, "Leadership is very much necessary, but people do not need to be dictated to! People need to have a voice and leaders need to be able to hear what the people are saying. People need leaders to keep them informed and mainly to be honest. People need leaders who are going to represent them and not going to play both sides of the fence. People want leaders whose yea will be yea, and their nay will be nay. They don't need leaders to say one thing and behind closed doors say another. People want leaders to be authentic."

Mr. Cunningham explained that it is not easy to get people to trust leaders because of unethical behaviors of past leaders. When someone is classified or regarded as a leader, they need to know how to deal with all types of individuals, the godly and the ungodly, in any situation. When bringing people together, Mr. Cunningham expressed the importance of being honest and allowing people to express their opinions concerning issues.

Mr. Cunningham works very well with the people in his organizations. First, he respects everyone and their opinions even when they may disagree with him. Secondly, he is a Christian man who believes in the Bible and who tries to live according to God's Word. He tries to live peaceably among men. Mr. Cunningham stated that in most instances, you must find mutual ground and meet there. Then, base your decision on what is best for the organization.

Mr. Cunningham is a pillar of the community in which he lives. He has many individuals come to him for assistance and advice. Mr. Cunningham sells used cars, but he tries to make sure that every customer is a satisfied customer. You can say he treats people the way he wants to be treated. Reared during an era where leaders were being killed, Mr. Cunningham said that watching what the Kennedys and King did motivated him to want to do more. Even when Dr. Martin Luther King, Jr. died, it didn't discourage him from continuing to do the right thing by all people. He said he felt progress was being made. He felt as if Dr. King made major accomplishments and there were others who could continue the movement. That's what instilled in him to press on. He said things have certainly improved from where they used to be.

My decision to interview Mr. Cunningham came as I passed his home one day, even after realizing I could interview any preacher, pastor, police officer, etc. For me, I wanted someone who has created change and overcome through change, and one who would not be afraid to say where they came from. I have had the opportunity to speak with Mr. Cunningham in various settings and have found out what type of person he is. He doesn't walk around like he is better than anyone but as one who has concern for others. I see his leadership abilities in his character inside and outside of the church. That is what motivated me to ask him if I could interview him as my change agent.

When I reflect on Mr. Cunningham, I see a man who beat the odds. Born into poverty, he didn't allow his circumstances to alter his destiny. Not only did he want better for himself, but also for those who he connected with. His ethical behavior and morals are what make him a force to be reckoned with. His humility, love and passion for others are seen in his walk and his talk.

Mr. Cunningham's style of leadership is a high supportive-low directive style or S3. He gives recognition and social support to subordinates. During this interview, I learned a lot about Mr. Cunningham that I would not have ever imagined. I learned what helped to mold him into the leader he has become and what it is that keeps him motivated. I learned that hard work pays off.

Mr. Cunningham held numerous jobs simultaneously to obtain financial stability. A good leader not only leads outside of his home but in his home as well. A leader never settles for anything less than what is expected. Sometimes you must leave people behind to move forward. Being a leader may come at a price that many aren't willing to pay. The most important thing I learned from Mr. Cunningham is that in his 78 years of life, he has seen a lot of different things. One thing that has never changed, though, is his desire for people to be treated fairly. His mantra remains, "always treat people the way you want to be treated."

Mr. Cunningham is a man who has gone from poverty to prosperity. He gives God all the glory for allowing him to first take a stand at the plant in Laurens, when it wasn't popular to stand and for using him as a leader to encourage others.

Giant

Dorinda Crawford

In reflecting on Black History Month which is celebrated during the month of February, I began to think about unsung heroes whose names do not appear in history books. These are people who for years have made a difference in the lives of others. These are people who generously share with others to give others a hand up. These are people who exemplify integrity. These are people who others in their community respect and admire.

In my reflection, it did not take me long to think of someone who could be graded A+ on all the above. That person is my cousin, businessman, civic/community leader and most of all Christian, Ulysses Cunningham. Even though he is my cousin, my comments about him are objective.

How does Ulysses make a difference in the lives of others? I am not allowed enough space in this publication to share it all. I will mention one example that will give a glimpse...Ulysses has three daughters. He sent all three of them to college. When the youngest daughter graduated from college, he and his wife Cora did not say, "We've educated our children. We ain't responsible for nobody else." Instead, they assisted in educating others. My daughter was one of the beneficiaries. They contributed so many funds to her education that I said to her, "When you graduate, you should give your degree to Ulysses and Cora because they put more into it than you did."

My daughter has graduated from college and now has a son in college. Ulysses has begun with the second generation of assistance by helping him financially in college. As Ulysses was writing a check for my grandson, he said to me, "When I was in college, someone from Laurens came to the college and gave me 25 cents. At that time 25 cents were a lot of money. It was really a lot of money for me because I was flat broke." Ulysses has never forgotten where he came from.

Ulysses gives people a hand up, not a hand out. For example, he gives a hand up to the unemployed by offering them odd jobs to make money. That's called teaching people how to fish to feed themselves. If that is not a hand up, then I don't know what is. I know someone whose car was out of whack and they did not have money to buy a new car. This left them with no way to get to work. Ulysses loaned the person a car so that they could get to their job. Helping someone get to work is a hand up.

Ulysses has a good reputation, but he defines integrity. Reputation is who people **think** you are. Integrity is who you are **when you think nobody is looking**. Ulysses sells used cars. If the car is not suitable for long distance travel, he will tell you that straight up before you buy the car. He'll even tell you what all is wrong with the car before you buy it. I've said on more than one occasion, Ulysses is the only used car dealer I trust.

Everyone in the community respects and admires Ulysses. Folks will tell you right off hand, 'Ulysses is a good man." I have never heard anyone in the community say anything bad about Ulysses. Now that may sound like a cliché, but it is what it is and it is true that I have never heard anyone say anything bad about the man.

Ulysses didn't write the quotation, but he does live it, "Some men see things as they are and say 'why?' I dream things that never were and say why not?"

A Classmate and Lifetime Friend

Lillie Beasley Glover, PhD., CFSC

Ulysses Cunningham and I have been friends since our days of matriculation at Sanders High School, Laurens, South Carolina. He was quiet and reserved. Throughout the years, our relationship has continued as our paths crossed in and out of Laurens as we planned for several successful Class Reunions, Sanders Grand Reunions, community/church activities, and special celebrations. Ulysses has always been a serious-minded individual who is highly self-motivated/directed, ambitious and committed to the concept of "improving the quality of life for individuals and families."

Ulysses has also evidenced outstanding human and material resource management skills; integrity; creativity and ingenuity when addressing pragmatic problems. He maintains excellent personal relations; working effectively independently as well as a team member, and he has a high level of enthusiasm. Ulysses readily assists with identified tasks in many areas and at times, goes the extra mile to ensure success. His successful career and subsequent retirement are evidence of his valued contribution to the community and society.

Faithful Deacon

Deacon Johnnie Cunningham

After serving in the United States Army, Deacon Ulysses Cunningham became very active at the Good Hope Baptist Church in Waterloo, South Carolina, around the year 1969. Deacon Ulysses attended Sunday School and worked very closely with Deacon John E. Calwise, who was the Chairman of the Deacon Board. In 1970, Deacon Ulysses became Chairman of the Board, and he continues to serve in this capacity. As Chairman of the Board of Deacons, Deacon Ulysses ensures that Good Hope stays within its budget. He is always active in the church's other auxiliaries, giving valuable input to their goals and objectives. As a member of the Executive Board, Deacon Ulysses serves Union Number Two of the Tumbling Shoals Baptist Association in Laurens, SC and serves as treasurer.

A Lifetime Friend & Church Member

Anna Pyles

I, Anna, have known Ulysses for a number of years, as far back to when he, his sisters and brothers, along with his mom and dad resided in Waterloo, SC. He has always been polite and a hard worker. This was even before he went off to college. He has been a member of Good Hope Baptist Church for many, many years, holding different positions: , Sunday School superintendent, cemetery attendant and now Chairman of the Board of Deacons. In these positions, Ulysses has made a great difference in church politics. He has listened and been fair with decisions, and he'll let you know his thoughts during the decision-making process.

A Former Supervisor and Friend

Jim Barton

I am honored to be asked to contribute my thoughts about Ulysses Cunningham who has been my gracious friend for many years. I am honored because he is an outstanding Christian, a caring and loving father, a great employee during his working days where our relationship began, a hard-working and dependable worker in his part-time jobs, and always ready and able to help a friend. There was never a doubt about him contributing less than 100%. Looking at his life and accomplishments now, it is easy to see that hard work, dedication, and desire to be successful has paid off for him.

He has shared with me the difficulties, the conditions, the heart aches, and the unknowns he experienced as a youngster growing up in Waterloo. He decided there had to be a better way through life. And I get chill bumps when I think about what he has accomplished in his life. He should be a model for all of us.

I felt that there was something special about him the first time I met him at work. I was a fairly new employee at the Laurens plant, but I had been spending a lot of time in Laurens as new products were transferring from the Chattanooga plant. The time came when additional Quality Control employees were needed and I thought Ulysses would fit that job. So, I recommended him for the job to the group that made the final decision. After some serious questions and discussions about his qualifications, the decision was made for me to offer him the job. It was an exciting discussion—he accepted the job before he knew what the job really was! And that was the start of using his abilities and talents where everybody no longer had any doubts about his capabilities as he progressed through 3M at more challenging positions.

I remember the time I asked him if he would like to join some of our other 3Mers at the old Darlington Street gym where we played volleyball after work. He looked surprised and suggested that I "check it out." Much to my surprise, I was told by one of the leading citizens in Laurens that it would be best if he did not join us. And he never joined our volleyball group, but now I am happy to see him at the YMCA exercising to keep healthy.

Over the years, he helped me buy cars and I helped him find cars to sell. He knew the car business and did very well in this business.

The highlight of our friendship for me was when he asked me to speak at his retirement dinner celebration. I left 3M in 1978. He made some changes as 3M sold the company to GE. I did not move from Laurens but I spent most of my time away from Laurens until I retired, so I did not see him often in those days. So, I was pleasantly surprised and pleased that he wanted me to say something at his retirement.

Now we are senior citizens and slowing down. I know for sure that the world and Laurens, South Carolina are better off because Ulysses Cunningham has spent some time right here. And I know that I am a better person because he spent some of that time with me.

I wish for Ulysses, Cora, the girls and the grandchildren the best life has to offer, and I thank you for this opportunity to say something about Ulysses.

Fast and True Friends

John Clemmons

Mr. Cunningham and I met over eight years ago. Our friendship took off like we had known each other all our lives. I'm so glad we became friends because he is a true friend. He is always a gentleman, kind, honest, generous and well-liked by all who cross his path.

Mr. C. has reared a wonderful family that adores him as much as he adores them. He is devoted to the Lord, his family and his church. He walks the walk.

I can call on Mr. C. at any time and he is there as I am for him. We know we can depend on each other. We talk several times a day and we are as close as brothers. He is special to me. Mr. C., I love you!

A Tribute to Ulysses Cunningham

Brenda Holland Curry

Mr. Ulysses Cunningham has been a friend of our family for numerous years. He and my uncle, the Late John W. Calhoun, were partners with their painting and car businesses.

Mr. Cunningham is a very soft spoken person, but when he speaks, others listen. There are many that seek advice from Mr. Cunningham, which demonstrates that he is a respected person in the community.

After I was elected a Commissioner for Laurens Commission of Public Works, Mr. Cunningham and I became friends. He has taught me a lot about our procedures, and he's always a phone call away when I need to ask a question, if I need a ride to a function, or if I need directions to a venue.

Mr. Cunningham is also a family man. He purchases vegetables from my husband and me, and he shares them with his children, sisters and friends. He also is one of the main caregivers for his mother-in-law.

William, my husband, and I love and respect Ulysses Cunningham, and we thank him for his love, friendship and concern for others.

The Mark of a Good Man

William Kilgore, Sr. (Punkin)

When we speak of good men, we look at their soul. This includes the way they carry themselves at all times. They always speak and act with good rapport towards everyone. When I speak of Mr. Cunningham, I see this quality. In fact, all the good qualities that make a good son, brother, husband, father, grandfather, neighbor and friend; I have found these things in him. Ulysses does not measure his importance by titles nor money. He uses the content of his character, the cleanliness of his speech, and the way he lives let everyone know that a godly man stands before them. The most glorious climax of all created things, for a true good man, is the human image of God. This is Ulysses Cunningham – my friend.

Ulysses Cunningham, A Friend to Man: The Story of a Soldier & Steward

Memorabilia

Letter from Dad to Mom from Germany in June of 1963

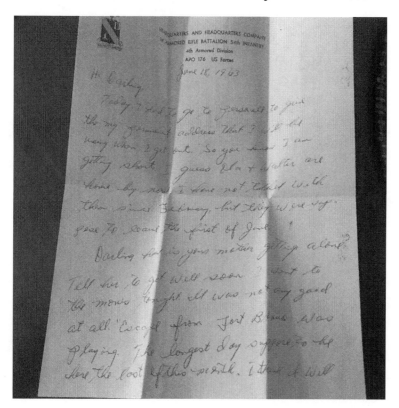

Letter from Germany Continued

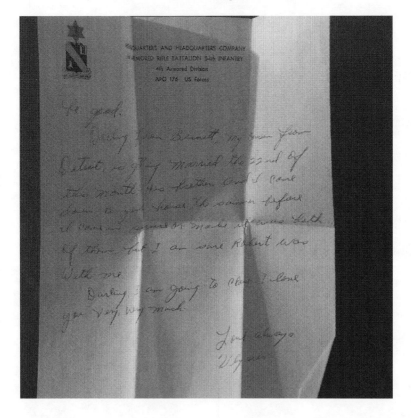

Envelope for Letter from Germany

Resume

Ulysses Cunningham
Route 5 Box 62
Laurens, SC 29360
(864) 984-5397

BUSINESS EXPERIENCE

1995 - Present — General Electric - Greenville, SC - Quality Control Specialist - Work station audits, CVP audits, final audits, initiate QCR's for operators and myself, close QCR's, tag scrap parts.

1995 - 1992 — GE Gas Turbine, Greenville, SC - Gage Lab Technician - Gage Calibration

1992 - 1990 — GE Gas Turbine, Greenville, SC - Worked a two year special assignment. I was responsible for shipping and receiving the correct buckets to and from coating at VPS. Keeping the right buckets in queue and filling in for supervisor when he was absent plus several other misc. duties.

1990 - 1989 — GE Gas Turbine, Greenville, SC - Quality control operator at Ardrox in the bucket area; L.P. buckets, workstation audits.

1989 - 1988 — Alsimag, Greenville, SC - Production Control Specialist Production scheduling; backlog analysis and control; system scheduling; queue list maintenance; expedite orders; update COMS/LMS; reorder tracking; product review planning; supply versus demand audits; shop order WIP control; critical body and supply control; shop order release; shop floor reporting control.

1988 - 1986 — General Electric Ceramics, Laurens, SC - Production Control Specialist - Production scheduling; backlog analysis and control; system scheduling; queue list maintenance; expedite orders; update COMS/LMS; reorder tracking; product review planning; supply versus demand audits; shop order WIP control; critical body and supply control; shop order release; Y.M. reports; shop floor reporting control.

1986 - 1985 — General Electric Ceramics Laurens, SC - Production Service Specialist - Provide information to field sales/customers with good accurate information very timely. Enter orders properly in COMS. Take customers orders orally, faxed and electronically.

1985 - 1983 — General Electric Ceramics Laurens, SC - Production Control Specialist - Work very closely with sales, manufacturing and other service groups expediting orders, materials and other necessary related services and/or equipment.
Member of Order Entry team for extruded ware. Checking for tooling, material, equipment and capacity. Responsible for six manufacturing departments as a Production Control Specialist, including shop loading, sequencing and recommending overtime to meet customer requirements.

1983 - 1972 — 3M Technical Ceramics - Dispatcher - Answer sales inquiries, line up department, schedule orders and expedite orders.

1972 - 1965 — 3M Technical Ceramics - Quality Auditor - Quality Control Supervisor

1965 - 1964 — 3M Technical Ceramics - Cast Tape Operator

1964 - 1963 — 3M Technical Ceramics - Custodian

1963 - 1961 — SP4 US Army - Assistance Squad Leader - Gunner on a 4.2 Mortar

1961 - 1960 — Standard Plywood's, Inc. - Clinton, SC - Plywood Grader

EDUCATION:

Lander College, Greenwood, SC
Graduation Date 1977
Degree: Business Administration

REFERENCES:

Professional references supplied upon request.

Ulysses Cunningham in the Quality Control Department, uses a projector with a 31.25 magnification to check the dimensional tolerances on a substrate. (Inset shows actual size of the substrate.)

Dad featured in *Impact*, Technical Education Magazine in SC
March 1972
Laurens, SC

**Retirement Program 1999
Clinton, SC**

In

Celebration & Recognition

of a

Life of Dedicated Service

for

Mr. Ulysses Cunningham

June 19, 1999
6:00 P.M.

Darlington House
Clinton, South Carolina

November 12, 2008

Photo by Daniel J. Lauer

CUNNINGHAM RENEWS HIS OATH — Ulysses Cunningham takes the oath of office for the Commission of Public Works on Monday. Cunningham was re-elected for district 1, seat 2, during last week's election with no opposition.

75th Birthday Celebration 2013
Laurens, SC

Photos

Dad's maternal grandmother, Betty Watts (back row right in striped
blouse) is pictured with her parents and siblings, a family of
sharecroppers in Waterloo, SC.
This photo was taken around 1875.

The Late Caleb Cunningham, Jr.,
Father of Ulysses

Approximately 8 Years Old
Laurel Hill Elementary School
Waterloo, SC

Senior Photo
Sanders High School Class of 1957
Laurens, SC

Ulysses Cunningham, A Friend to Man: The Story of a Soldier & Steward

At home in 1957
Laurens, SC

Dad

Sanders High School Class of 1957
Laurens, SC

Advanced to E2
1962
Fort Gordon, Georgia

1962
Fort Gordon, Georgia

Dad

US Army
1963
Heilbronn, Germany

Dad after being honorably discharged from the US Army in 1964.
Laurens, SC

Dad holding Toni as an infant in front of the family home in 1966.
Laurens, SC

Dad holding Sonia with Toni and Shae at his side
May 1970
Philadelphia, Pennsylvania

Dad with Cora, Toni, Shae, Sonia and brother-in-law,
The Late Dicky Barksdale
1972
Disney World, Orlando, Florida

Dad and Toni
January 1988
Laurens, SC

Dad and Shae
February 1992
Laurens, SC

Dad and Sonia
December 1993
Laurens, S

Dad and Chris
December 1990
Laurens, SC

Dad and Jasmine
September 1994
Laurens, SC

Dad and BJ
August 1996
Laurens, SC

Dad and Jalen
September 2000
Simpsonville, SC

Ulysses Cunningham, A Friend to Man: The Story of a Soldier & Steward

Mom and Dad Before the NAACP Banquet
January 1998
Laurens, SC

Dad's 50th Class Reunion
May 2007
Clinton, SC

Dad Outside His Office
2009
Laurens, SC

Dad and Family
Memorial Day 2010
Anderson, SC

Mom's 70th Birthday Celebration
June 2012
Laurens, SC

Dad and Shae
May 2013
Anderson, SC

Dad's 75th Birthday Celebration
December 2013
Laurens, SC

Dad and Family
Christmas 2014
Simpsonville, SC

Ulysses Cunningham, A Friend to Man: The Story of a Soldier & Steward

Dad and Carolina Auto Auction Employee
Dealer of the Week
April 22, 2015
Anderson, SC

Dad and Sonia
Friendship AME Women of Excellence Recognition
March 2017
Clinton, SC

About the Author

Dr. Sonia Cunningham Leverette

Passionate about creating tomorrow's leaders, Amazon Best-Selling Author Dr. Sonia Cunningham Leverette is a lifelong writer and language arts teacher. She combines her love for humanity with books. Wife, mother and veteran educator with almost thirty years of experience, Dr. Leverette focuses extensively on enlightening, empowering and educating through her publications. *Ulysses Cunningham A Friend to Man: The Story of a Soldier and Steward* is her first biography, and she enlisted the assistance of her father, for whose life the book is written, her sisters Toni Cunningham Smith and Sabrina Cunningham Thomas, who are also veteran educators, and a host of other family members, friends and community members.

Dr. Leverette's children's books, *BJ's Big Dream, He Never Slumbers, What is That Stinky, Winky Eeewww Smell?* and *My Friends Lived in the Outlet* address self-esteem, self-confidence and goal-setting.

For bulk sales, author visits, speaking engagements and publishing opportunities, visit soniacunninghamleverette.com. The author can be reached via email at soncunnlev@gmail.com.

Ulysses Cunningham, A Friend to Man: The Story of a Soldier & Steward

86663945R00083

Made in the USA
Columbia, SC
17 January 2018